Printed in China

“漫画汉语 101 句”
系列丛书策划

周明伟　黄友义　徐明强
王君校　韩　晖

Chinese 101 in Cartoons

(For Shopping)

漫画汉语101句

（购物篇）

侯　琨 史文华 编著

韩芙芸 译

千秋叶工作室 插图

华语教学出版社

SINOLINGUA

First Edition 2011

ISBN 978-7-80200-938-7

Published by Sinolingua Co., Ltd.
24 Baiwanzhuang Road, Beijing 100037, China
Tel: (86) 10-68320585
Fax: (86) 10-68326333
http://www.sinolingua.com.cn
E-mail: hyjx@sinolingua.com.cn
Printed by Beijing Foreign Languages Printing House

Printed in the People's Republic of China

Preface

In recent years an increasing number of foreign friends are beginning to pay attention to China. They are eager to know more about the country and communicate further with the Chinese people. The number of foreigners learning Chinese throughout the world is increasing on a yearly basis and "Chinese fever" is gaining momentum. Yet due to limitations of time and learning conditions, a large number of foreigners who want to learn Chinese still have no access to regular and professional training. There are also many people who simply give up because of the degree of difficulty involved. To resolve these problems and help assist those who basically have no knowledge of Chinese to master some words and expressions for everyday use, we have carefully designed this series, titled *Chinese 101 in Cartoons.*

Each book in this series is designed to cater to the various needs of different people. The 101 expressions selected are all used frequently in daily conversation. The series mainly has two features: the lively and colorful cartoons which help readers better understand the conversational scenes; the recording of standardized Mandarin Chinese, which is necessary to help develop the correct pronunciation. There is no obscure grammar here, and readers need not memorize the strokes of the Chinese characters. All they need to do is to imagine the scene with the aid of the cartoon, try to memorize the Chinese sentence with the help of the English translation, and pronounce it with the help of the pinyin and the recording.

In addition, there are many word options that can serve as substitutes for those in the 101 commonly used sentence patterns presented in each book. The learners thus can draw inferences about other sentences from any given example. There are lively and humorous tips with cartoons that introduce Chinese customs and culture, and also explain differences between the East and the West.

Catchy and lively Chinese conversation starts from *Chinese 101 in Cartoons*. With one book on hand, you can proudly say: "I can speak Chinese!"

前言

近年来，越来越多的外国友人开始关注中国，希望了解中国，渴望与中国人交流。在世界各地，学习汉语的外国人正逐年增加，“汉语热”持续升温。由于时间、条件等的限制，许多有学习汉语愿望的外国人目前无法在学校接受正规、系统的课堂教学；也有一些外国人认为汉语这门古老的语言难学、难记，难以掌握，对此望而却步。为了解决这些问题，帮助更多汉语为零起点的外国人学习一些简单的日常用语，我们精心策划了这套“漫画汉语 101 句”系列丛书。

丛书每册根据不同人群的不同需求分别编写，均选取日常会话中使用频率较高的 101 句话教给读者。以轻松活泼的彩色漫画形式帮助读者理解会话场景、以标准的普通话录音帮助读者模仿发音是本书最大的特色。在这里，没有生涩难懂的语法，不需要熟记汉字笔画，只需借助画面进入情境、根据与中文句子对应的英文理解意思、对照汉语拼音读出发音就可以了。

另外，每册书提供的 101 句常用句式同时给出了多种可替换词语，学习者可以举一反三，一句衍生多句。书中更有生动幽默、配漫画的小贴士介绍中国的风俗习惯、文化常识，以及中外差异趣闻等，帮助读者了解中国。

简单易学、生动有趣的汉语，从“漫画汉语 101 句”开始。一书在手，你就可以骄傲地说：我会说汉语了！

Key to Pronunciation

Beginning Consonants

b	*b* as in *be*
c	*ts* as in *tsar*, strongly aspirated
d	*d* as in *do*
f	*f* as in *food*
g	*g* as in *go*
h	*h* as in *her*
j	*j* as in *jeep*
k	*k* as in *kind*
l	*l* as in *land*
m	*m* as in *man*
n	*n* as in *nine*
p	*p* as in *par*
q	*ch* as in *cheek*
r	like *z* in *azure*
s	*s* as in *sister*
t	*t* as in *ten*
w	*w* as in *way*
x	*sh* as in *she*

y	*y* as in *yet*
z	*ds* as in *needs*
zh	*j* as in *jump*
ch	*ch* as in *church*
sh	*sh* as in *shore*

Vowels and Diphthongs

a	*a* as in *father*
ai	*i* as in *kite*
ao	*ow* as in *now*
an	*ahn*
ang	like *ong* in *song*
e	*er* as in *her* (Brit.)
ei	*ay* as in *way*
en	weak form of *an* as in *and*
eng	no English equivalent but nearly as *ung* in *lung*
i	*ea* as in *eat*
ia	*yah*
ie	*ye* as in *yes*
iao	*yow* as in *yowl*
iou	*yee-oh*

ian	*ien* as in *lenient*
in	*een* as in *keen*
iang	*i-ahng*
ing	*ing* as in *sing*
iong	*y-oong*
o	*aw* as in *law*
ou	*ow* as in *low*
ong	*oo-ng*
u	*oo* as in *too*
ua	*wah*
uo	*wa* as in *water*
uai	*wi* as in *wife*
uei	as *way*
uan	*oo-ahn*
uen	*won* as in *wonder*
uang	*oo-ahng*
ueng	*won* as in *wont*
ü*	as "*yü*" in German
üe	no English equivalent
üan	no English equivalent
ün	no English equivalent

---

* "ü" is spelt so only when it follows "l" and "n", otherwise it is spelt as "u".

目录

Contents

UNIT 1

Càishìchǎng (Yī)

菜市场（一）

At a Vegetable Market (I)

Shūcàitān
（蔬菜摊 At a Vegetable Stall）

Coco： Nǐ hǎo.
① Coco：你 好。

Coco: Hello!

Tānzhǔ： Nín hǎo. Nín mǎi shénme?
摊主：您 好。您 买 什么？

Vendor: Hello! What would you like to buy?

Coco： Húluóbo duōshao qián yì jīn？
② Coco：胡萝卜多少钱一斤？

Coco: How much is a *jin* of carrots?

Huángguā
黄瓜 cucumbers
Tǔdòu
土豆 potatoes
Yángcōng
洋葱 onions
Xīhóngshì
西红柿 tomatoes
Mógu
蘑菇 mushrooms
Qiézi
茄子 eggplants
Biǎndòu
扁豆 lentils
Báicài
白菜 Chinese cabbages
Qíncài
芹菜 celery
Hóngshǔ
红薯 sweet potatoes

Tānzhǔ： Bā máo qián yì jīn.
摊主：8毛钱一斤。

Vendor: Eight *mao* for one *jin*.

Liǎng kuài qián
两块钱 Two *kuai*
Liǎng kuài wǔ
两块五 Two and fifty *kuai*

Tānzhǔ : Nín mǎi duōshao ?
摊主：您 买 多少？

Vendor: How much would you like?

Coco : Wǒ mǎi liǎng jīn .
③ Coco：我 买 两 斤。

Coco: Two *jin* please.

sān jīn
三斤 Three *jin*
yìdiǎnr
一点儿 A little bit

Shuǐguǒ tān
（水果摊 At a Fruit Stall）

Tānzhǔ : Lái diǎnr shuǐguǒ ba .
摊主：来点儿水果吧。
Vendor: Would you like some fruit?

Coco : Wǒ mǎi yì jīn xiāngjiāo .
④ Coco：我买一斤香蕉。
Coco: I'll take one *jin* of bananas.

píngguǒ
苹果 apples
chéngzi
橙子 oranges
mángguǒ
芒果 mangoes
níngméng
柠檬 lemons
táozi
桃子 peaches
pútao
葡萄 grapes
yīngtáo
樱桃 cherries
cǎoméi
草莓 strawberries
míhóutáo
猕猴桃 kiwi fruit
dàzǎo
大枣 dates

Tānzhǔ : Hái mǎi shénme?
摊主：还买什么？

Vendor: Anything else?

Coco : Wǒ hái yào yí gè xīguā .
⑤ Coco：我还要一个西瓜。

Coco: Also a water melon.

yòuzi
柚子 pomelo
bōluó
菠萝 pineapple
hāmìguā
哈密瓜 Hami melon
liúlián
榴莲 durian

Tānzhǔ :　Hái yào biéde ma ?
摊主：还要别的吗？

Vendor: Anything else?

Coco　:　Bú yào le .
⑥ Coco：不要了。

Coco: No, that's all.

Coco： Yígòng duōshao qián?
⑦ Coco：一共 多少 钱？

Coco: How much is the total?

Tānzhǔ： Yígòng shíqī kuài.
摊主：一共 17 块。

Vendor: 17 yuan please.

Coco : Gěi nǐ qián .
⑧ Coco：给你钱。

Coco: Here you are.

Tānzhǔ : Zhǎo nín sān kuài .
摊主：找您 3 块。

Vendor: Here is three yuan for your change.

Tips 1

Chinese Currency

The units of the Renminbi are the yuan (*kuai* in oral language), *jiao* (*mao* in oral language) and *fen*. One yuan is equal to 10 *jiao*, and 1 *jiao* is equal to 10 *fen*.

UNIT 2

Càishìchǎng (Èr)

菜市场（二）

At a Vegetable Market (II)

Tānzhǔ : Nín yào shénme ròu , lǐji , hòutuǐ , niúnǎn háishi niúshàngnǎo?
摊主：您要什么肉，里脊、后腿、牛腩还是牛上脑？

Vendor: What kind of meat would you like, tenderloin, rump, hanger or blade?

Coco : Wǒ zuò niúpái , mǎi lǐji ba .
⑨ Coco：我做牛排，买里脊吧。

Coco: I'd like to cook beefsteak, so tenderloin please.

Coco : Yǒu lǐyú ma?
⑩ Coco：有鲤鱼吗？

Coco: Do you have any carp?

jìyú
鲫鱼 crucian
niányú
鲇鱼 catfish

Tānzhǔ : Yǒu, dōu shì huó de.
摊主：有，都是活的。

Vendor: Yes, they are all alive.

Coco ： Gěi wǒ yì tiáo xiǎo yìdiǎnr de .
⑪ Coco：给我一条小一点儿的。

Coco: I'll take a small one.

dà
大 big

Tānzhǔ ： Zhè tiáo zěnmeyàng ？
摊主：这条怎么样？

Vendor: How about this one?

Coco : Bāng wǒ qīnglǐ yíxiàr , kěyǐ ma?
⑫ Coco：帮我清理一下儿，可以吗？

Coco: Would you please prepare it for me?

shōushi
收拾 get it ready
qiē
切 cut it

Tānzhǔ : Méi wèntí .
摊主：没问题。

Vendor: No problem.

Coco : Xièxie , zàijiàn .
⑬ Coco：谢谢，再见。

Coco: Thanks, bye.

Tānzhǔ : Bú kèqi . Xià cì zài lái .
摊主：不客气。下次再来。

Vendor: You are welcome. Please come again.

Tips 2

Chinese Vegetable Markets
The vegetable markets, either big or small, are located in the communities. They also provide daily necessities besides fresh fruit and vegetables, fish and meat. Things there are usually cheaper than those in the supermarkets, and you are also free to haggle for a better price.

UNIT 3

Cháyè diàn
茶叶店
At a Tea Store

Diànyuán : Xīn dào de cháyè , huānyíng pǐncháng .
店员 ：新到的茶叶， 欢迎 品尝 。

Salesperson: This tea is a new arrival. Please try some.

Coco : Wèidào búcuò .
⑭ Coco：味道 不错。

Coco: It tastes pretty good.

Coco : Wǒ xiǎng yào tiěguānyīn .
⑮ Coco：我 想 要 铁观音。

Coco: I'd like some Tieguanyin tea.

lóngjǐngchá
龙井茶 Dragon Well tea
pǔ'ěrchá
普洱茶 Pu'er tea
wūlóngchá
乌龙茶 Oolong tea
hóngchá
红茶 black tea
huāchá
花茶 scented tea

Diànyuán : Zhè zhǒng yuánjià yìbǎiliù ,
店员：这 种 原价一百六，
xiànzài bànjià , bāshí .
现在 半价，八十。

Salesperson: This one was previously 160 yuan, but now we offer a 50% discount.

Coco : Xiān yào èr liǎng chángchang ba .
⑯ Coco：先要二两 尝尝 吧。

Coco: I'll take two *liang* to start.

Diànyuán : Xià cì nín kěyǐ chángchang nà zhǒng , yě hěn hǎo .
店员：下次您可以 尝尝 那种，也很好。

Salesperson: You may try that one next time. It's good, too.

Coco ： Xíng . Zài gěi pèi ge cháyètǒng ba .
⑰ Coco ：行。再给配个茶叶筒吧。

Coco: Okay. Please put it into a tea can.

Diànyuán ： Zǒnggòng wǔshí kuài .
店员 ： 总共 50 块。

Salesperson: The total is 50 *kuai*.

Coco： Qián zhènghǎo. Zàijiàn.
⑱ Coco：钱 正好。再见。

Coco: I have the exact change. Goodbye.

Diànyuán： Zàijiàn. Nín màn zǒu.
店员：再见。您慢走。

Salesperson: Goodbye. Take care.

Tips 3

Seasons and Tea Drinking

Chinese tea is divided into various types, and their tastes and functions differ greatly. Spring is the season for scented tea, which expels the coldness accumulated in the body over winter and lifts the spirit from drowsiness. Summer is the season for green tea, whose cooling nature can counter the summer heat and strengthen health; while autumn is the season for oolong tea, which can moisturize the skin, moisten the throat and boost the secretion of saliva. Winter is the season for black tea, and its hot nature helps protect the body against winter chills.

UNIT 4

Shāngchéng (Yī)
商城（一）
At a Shopping Mall (I)

Shòuhuòyuán : Huānyíng guānglín .
售货员 ： 欢迎 光临 。

Salesperson: Welcome to our shopping mall.

Coco : Wǒ suíbiàn kànkan .
⑲ Coco ： 我 随便 看看 。

Coco: I'm just looking around.

Coco ： Wǒ néng shìshi zhè shuāng xié ma？
⑳ Coco：我能试试这双鞋吗？

Coco: Can I try on this pair of shoes?

píxié
皮鞋 leather shoes
yùndòngxié
运动鞋 sports shoes
liángxié
凉鞋 sandals
xuēzi
靴子 boots

Shòuhuòyuán ： Dāngrán！ Nín chuān duō dà hào de？
售货员：当然！您穿多大号的？

Salesperson: Of course. What is your size?

Coco : Wǒ chuān sānshíbā hào de .
㉑ Coco：我 穿 38 号的。

Coco: Size 38 please.

Shòuhuòyuán : Gěi nín . Zhèr yǒu jìngzi .
售货员 ：给 您。这儿有 镜子。

Salesperson: Here you are. The mirror is here.

Coco： Yǒudiǎnr dà， qǐng huàn yì shuāng .
㉒ Coco：有点儿大，请 换 一 双 。

xiǎo
小 small

Coco: They're a bit large. Please bring another pair.

Shòuhuòyuán： Nín shìshi zhè shuāng .
售货员 ：您试试这 双 。

Salesperson: You can try on this pair.

Coco ： Zhège hěn héshì ． Dǎzhé ma？
㉓ Coco：这个很合适。打折吗？

Coco: They fit well. Is there a discount?

Shòuhuòyuán： Dǎ wán zhé yǐhòu sānbǎi kuài．
售货员 ：打完折以后 300 块。

Salesperson: They cost 300 *kuai* after a discount.

Coco : Nǐ kànkan wǒ zài zhèr mǎi de xié , chuānle jǐ tiān
㉔ Coco：你看看 我在这儿买的鞋，穿了 几天
jiù pò le .
就破了。

kāi xiàn
开线 split
kāi jiāo
开胶 delaminate

Coco: The shoes I bought here began to wear out after only a few days.

Shòuhuòyuán : Duìbuqǐ . Wǒmen gěi nín huàn yì shuāng .
售货员 ：对不起。我们 给 您 换 一 双 。

Salesperson: Sorry. I'll exchange for you.

Tips 4

Conversion Chart for Chinese and Foreign Shoe Sizes

Men's shoe size														
Foot Length (cm)	24.5	25	25.5	26	26.5	27	27.5	28	28.5	29	29.5	30	30.5	31
China	39	40	40.5	41	42	42.5	43	44	44.5	45	45.5	46	47	47.5
U. S.	6.5	7	7.5	8	8.5	9	9.5	10	10.5	11	11.5	12	12.5	13
England	5.5	6	6.5	7	7.5	8	8.5	9	9.5	10	10.5	11	11.5	12
Europe	39	40	40.5	41	42	42.5	43	44	44.5	45	45.5	46	47	47.5

Women's shoe size														
Foot Length (cm)	22.5	23	23.5	24	24.5	25	25.5	26	26.5	27	27.5	28	28.5	29
China	36	36.5	37.5	38	38.5	39	40	40.5	41	42	42.5	43	44	44.5
U. S.	5.5	6	6.5	7	7.5	8	8.5	9	9.5	10	10.5	11	11.5	12
England	3	3.5	4	4.5	5	5.5	6	6.5	7	7.5	8	8.5	9	9.5
Europe	36	36.5	37.5	38	38.5	39	40	40.5	41	42	42.5	43	44	44.5

UNIT 5

Shāngchéng (Èr)
商城（二）
At a Shopping Mall (II)

Coco : Wǒ xiǎng shìshi nà jiàn qípáo .
㉕ Coco：我 想 试试那件旗袍。

Coco: I'd like to try on that cheongsam.

chènyī
衬衣 shirt
T-xù
T 恤 T-shirt
máoyī
毛衣 sweater
wàitào
外套 coat

Shòuhuòyuán : Hǎo , shìyījiān zài zhèbian .
售货员 ：好，试衣间在这边。

Salesperson: Okay. The fitting room is here.

Coco : Tài féi le .
㉖ Coco ：太肥了。

shòu
瘦 tight

Coco: It's too loose.

Shòuhuòyuán : Gěi nín huàn ge hào shìshi ba ?
售货员 ：给您 换 个 号 试试吧？

Salesperson: I'll change the size for you.

Coco ： Wǒ bú yào le ， xièxie .
㉗ Coco：我 不要了，谢谢。

Coco: I don’t want it. Thanks.

Shòuhuòyuán： Nín zài kànkan qítā de .
售货员 ：您 再 看看其他的。

Salesperson: Please have a look at the other items.

Coco : Wǒ xiǎng gěi wǒ xiānsheng mǎi tiáo kùzi .
㉘ Coco：我 想 给我 先生 买 条 裤子。

Coco: I would like to buy a pair of trousers for my husband.

niúzǎikù
牛仔裤 jeans
yùndòngkù
运动裤 sports pants
duǎnkù
短裤 shorts

Shòuhuòyuán : Hǎo a . Nánzhuāng zài zhèbian .
售货员：好啊。男 装 在 这边。

Salesperson: Okay. Menswear is over here.

Coco : Zhè tiáo ba .
㉙ Coco：这 条吧。

Coco: I'll take this one.

Shòuhuòyuán : Hǎo . Bù héshì kěyǐ lái huàn .
售货员 ：好。不合适可以来换。

Salesperson: Okay. Please come for an exchange if it doesn't fit.

Coco： Qiántiān wǒ zài zhèr gěi wǒ xiānsheng mǎi de yīfu

㉚ Coco：前天 我在这儿给 我 先生 买的衣服

tài xiǎo le .

太小了。

dà 大 large

féi 肥 loose

shòu 瘦 tight

Coco: The clothes I bought here for my husband the day before yesterday are too small.

Shòuhuòyuán： Wǒ gěi nín huàn yí jiàn .

售货员 ：我 给 您 换 一件。

Salesperson: I'll exchange for you.

Shòuhuòyuán : Zhège shì tèjià shāngpǐn , bù néng tuì huàn .
售货员 ：这个是特价 商品 ，不 能 退换 。

Salesperson: This is a special offer and is non-refundable.

Coco : Rúguǒ bú tuì , wǒ jiù tóusù nǐmen .
㉛ Coco：如果不退，我就投诉你们。

Coco: If you don't give me a refund, I'll make a complaint.

Tips 5

Complaints

If you are unsatisfied with any purchased goods, you can ask for a refund or replacement. If the store unreasonably refuses to do so, you can make a complaint by calling the consumer association's hotline number, 12315, and telling them what happened. To have the problem solved more expediently, please keep all the invoices or purchase slips. Of course, it is better to ask whether the goods are refundable or not before purchasing them.

UNIT 6

Zhìyīdiàn

制衣店

At a Dressmaker's Shop

Coco : Wǒ xiǎng dìngzuò yí jiàn qípáo .
㉜ Coco：我 想 定做一件旗袍。

Coco: I'd like a made-to-measure cheongsam.

Cáifeng : Qǐng nín tiāoxuǎn yíxià bùliào .
裁缝 ：请 您 挑选 一下布料。

Dressmaker: Please select a fabric.

Coco ： Zhè zhǒng zhēnsī shuāngzhòu de zěnmeyàng?
㉝ Coco：这 种 真丝 双绉 的怎么样？

Coco: How about silk crepe de chine?

fǔchóu
府绸 poplin
gòngduàn
贡 缎 satin
chúnmián
纯 棉 cotton
xiāngyúnshā
香云纱 watered gauz

Cáifeng : Hěn hǎo a , nín xuǎn ge yàngzi ba .
裁缝 ：很 好啊，您 选 个样子吧。

Dressmaker: It's very good. Please choose a style.

Coco : Zhè kuǎn hěn piàoliang , wǒ xǐhuan .
㉞ Coco：这款很漂亮，我喜欢。

Coco: This is very pretty. I like it.

dàfang
大方 of good taste
diǎnyǎ
典雅 elegant
shìhé wǒ
适合我 suitable for me

Cáifeng : Bùliào sānbǎi kuài , réngōng èrbǎi kuài , yígòng wǔbǎi kuài .
裁缝：布料 300 块，人工 200 块，一共 500 块。

Dressmaker: The fabric costs 300 *kuai*, plus 200 *kuai* for the tailoring, so the total will be 500 *kuai*.

Coco : Tàiguì le , piányi diǎnr .
㉟ Coco：太贵了，便宜点儿。

Coco: That's too expensive. Can you make it cheaper?

Cáifeng : Bùliào kěyǐ dǎ jiǔ zhé , zuìdī èrbǎi qīshí kuài .
裁缝：布料可以打九折，最低 270 块。

Dressmaker: I can give you a 10% discount on the fabric, which will be 270 *kuai*.

Coco : Èrbǎi wǔshí kuài , xíngma ?
㊱ Coco : 250 块，行吗？

Coco: Will 250 *kuai* be okay?

Cáifeng : Èrbǎiwǔ shì shǎshù , èrbǎiliù ba .
裁缝 : 250 是傻数， 260 吧。

Dressmaker: 250 is a stupid number. Let's make it 260.

Coco : Jiù zhème dìng le .
㊲ Coco：就这么 定 了。

Coco: It's a deal.

Cáifeng : Wǒ gěi nín liáng yíxià chǐcùn .
裁缝：我 给 您 量 一下 尺寸。

Dressmaker: I'll measure you.

Tips 6

Numbers with a Meaning

Chinese people often use the number 250 to refer to people who do things in a careless and offhand way, and who cannot be relied upon. Thus, people often avoid using it. Lucky numbers include six, eight, nine, etc. Six represents good luck, eight represents prosperity and nine represents longevity.

UNIT 1

Jiādiànchéng

家电城

At a Home Appliance Store

Dǎogòu xiǎojiě： Nín hǎo， xiǎng mǎi shénme diànqì？
导购 小姐：您 好，想 买 什么 电器？

Saleslady: Hello. What would you like?

Coco： Wǒ xiǎng kànkan xiǎo jiādiàn.
㊳ Coco：我 想 看看 小 家电。

Coco: I'd like to have a look at the small appliances.

xǐyījī
洗衣机 washing machines

diànshìjī
电视机 televisions

kōngtiáo
空调 air conditioners

bīngxiāng
冰箱 refrigerators

Coco ： Zhè kuǎn wēibōlú zhìliàng zěnmeyàng？
㊴ Coco：这 款 微波炉 质量 怎么样？

Coco: Is this microwave oven of good quality?

miànbāojī
面包机 toaster
zhàzhījī
榨汁机 juice extractor
diànkǎoxiāng
电烤箱 electric oven
kāfēihú
咖啡壶 coffee pot
jiāshīqì
加湿器 humidifier

Dǎogòu xiǎojiě ： Fēicháng hǎo， bāo nín mǎnyì．
导购 小姐：非常 好，包 您 满意。

Saleslady: Yes, it's very good and you will be very satisfied.

Coco : Shì Zhōngguó zhìzào de ma?
⑩ Coco：是 中国 制造的吗？

Coco: Is it made in China?

Dǎogòu xiǎojiě : Dāngrán, háishi Zhōngguó míngpái ne,
导购 小姐：当然，还是 中国 名牌 呢，
wùměi-jiàlián.
物美价廉。

Saleslady: Of course. It's a famous Chinese brand that are known for their high quality and low prices.

Coco： Bǎoxiūqī duō cháng?
㊶ Coco：保修期 多 长？

Coco: How long is the warranty?

Dǎogòu xiǎojiě： Yì nián bǎoxiū， zhōngshēn wéihù.
导购 小姐：一年保修， 终身 维护。

Saleslady: It has a one year warranty for durable maintenance and repairs.

Tips 1

Business Hours of Chinese Stores

The shopping malls and supermarkets in China are generally open from 9 am to 10 pm, and do not close on the weekends and on public holidays. During some peak shopping days promotional activities will usually be arranged.

UNIT 8

Chāoshì
超市
At a Supermarket

Shōuyínyuán : Nín hǎo . Yǒu huìyuánkǎ ma?
收银员 ：您 好。有 会员卡 吗？

Cashier: Hello. Do you have a membership card?

Coco : Méiyǒu .
42 Coco ：没有 。

Coco: No, I don't.

Shōuyínyuán： Yào dàizi ma？
收银员 ：要袋子吗？

Cashier: Do you need a bag?

Coco ： Bú yòng， wǒ zìjǐ dài le .
㊸ Coco：不用，我自己带了。

Coco: No, I have one with me.

Coco : Dàizi mǎn le . Zài mǎi ge gòuwùdài ba .
㊹ Coco：袋子满了。再买个购物袋吧。

Coco: It is full. Could you please give me a shopping bag?

sùliàodài
塑料袋 plastic bag

Shōuyínyuán : Gòuwùdài sān kuài , sùliàodài wǔ máo .
收银员：购物袋 3 块，塑料袋 5 毛。

Cashier: A shopping bag costs three *kuai* and a plastic one costs five *mao*.

Shōuyínyuán : Shuā kǎ háishi jiāo xiànjīn ?
收银员 ：刷卡还是交现金？

Cashier: Do you want to pay by card or cash?

Coco : Shuā kǎ .
45 Coco：刷卡。

Coco: By card.

Shōuyínyuán : Qǐng shūrù mìmǎ . ... Zài zhèr qiān zì .
收银员 ：请输入密码。……在这儿签字。
Kǎ shōuhǎo .
卡收好。

Cashier: Please input your password.… Sign here and keep your card.

Coco : Hǎo de . Xièxie .
㊻ Coco：好的。谢谢。

Coco: Okay. Thanks.

Coco : Kāi fāpiào shì zài zhèli ma?
㊼ Coco : 开发票是在这里吗?

Tuì huò
退货 return the goods
Huàn huò
换货 replace the goods

Coco: Can I get a receipt here?

Shōuyínyuán : Bù , zài dìxià yī lóu zǒngfúwùtái .
收银员 : 不，在地下 1 楼总服务台。

Cashier: No. Please go down to the Service Counter on the basement floor.

Coco : zhège wǒ mǎi duō le , xiǎng tuì le .
⑱ Coco：这个我买多了，想退了。

chóng le
重了 twice
cuò le
错了 mistakenly

Coco: I bought it too many.
Can I return it?

Gōngzuò rényuán : Qǐng chūshì nín de xiǎopiào .
工作人员：请出示您的小票。
Staff: Please show me your purchase slip.

Tips 8

The Brand Supermarkets in Beijing

Big and small supermarkets are scattered everywhere around Beijing. These include world famous ones like Walmart, Carrefour, Auchan, Jenny Lou's and Lotus, etc., as well as local brands like Wu Mart, Jingkelong, Jian Mart, Merry Mart, Shuntianfu Supermarket and Chaoshifa, etc., where people can get food, clothing and other daily items.

UNIT 9

Xiǎoshāngpǐn Pīfā Shìchǎng

小商品 批发 市场

At a Small Commodities Wholesale Market

Diànzhǔ : Nín xūyào diǎnr shénme?
店主 ：您需要点儿什么？
Seller: What would you like?

Coco : Máotǎn yǒu shuāngrén de ma?
㊾ Coco ：毛毯有 双 人的吗？
Coco: Do you have a double blanket?

Chuángdān
床单 sheet
Bèitào
被套 duvet cover
Miánbèi
棉被 quilt

Diànzhǔ : Gěi nín zhège .
店主 ：给您这个。

Seller: Here you are.

Coco : Máfan nǐ bāng wǒ ná ge zuìhǎo de .
50 Coco ：麻烦你帮我拿个<u>最好</u>的。

Coco: Could you please get me the <u>best</u> one.

zuì hòu
最厚 thickest
chúnmián
纯棉 cotton

Diànzhǔ： Nín xǐhuan shénme yánsè de？
店主：您喜欢什么颜色的？

Seller: What color do you like?

Coco： Wǒ xǐhuan huángsè de．
51 Coco：我喜欢黄色的。

Coco: I like yellow.

hóngsè
红色 red
lǜsè
绿色 green
lánsè
蓝色 blue
júsè
橘色 orange
zōngsè
棕色 brown
huīsè
灰色 grey
báisè
白色 white
hēisè
黑色 black

Diànzhǔ : Zhège tú'àn nín xǐhuan ma?
店主 : 这个图案您 喜欢 吗?

Seller: Do you like this pattern?

Coco : Suìhuā tú'àn hěn hǎokàn , mǎi le .
52 Coco : 碎花图案很 好看, 买了。

Coco: Small Flowers is fine. I'll take it.

Gézi
格子 Checks
Dàhuā
大花 Big flowers
Tiáowén
条纹 Stripes

Coco : Zuò chuānglián duōshao jiāgōngfèi ?
53 Coco：做 窗帘 多少 加工费？

Coco: How much do you charge
for making a curtain?

yǐtào
椅套 chair cover
shāfātào
沙发套 slipcover

Diànzhǔ : Zài zhèr mǎi bù , miǎn jiāgōngfèi .
店主：在这儿买布，免 加工费。

Seller: It is free if you buy the fabric here.

Coco : Kěyǐ shàng mén ānzhuāng ma?
54 Coco：可以上门安装吗？

cèliáng
测量 measure

Coco: Could you install it at my house for me?

Diànzhǔ : Kěyǐ.
店主：可以。

Seller: Sure.

Coco : Yào ānzhuāng fèi ma ?
⑸ Coco：要 安装 费吗？

shàngmén
上门 onsite service

Coco: Will you charge for the installation?

Diànzhǔ : Hēhe , miǎn fèi de .
店主：呵呵， 免 费的。

Seller: Haha, it's free.

Diànzhǔ : Nín de dìzhǐ hé diànhuà shì shéme ?
店主：您的地址和电话是什么？

Seller: Would you please give me your address and phone number?

Coco : Xìngfú Xiǎoqū yī hàolóu sì líng èr . Diànhuà shì
56 Coco：幸福小区1号楼402。电话是
liùbājiǔjiǔ x x x x .
6899××××。

Coco: Room 402, Building No.1, Xingfu District. My phone number is 6899….

Coco ： Qǐngwèn， néng shuā kǎ ma？
57 Coco ： 请问 ， 能 刷 卡吗？

Coco: Excuse me, can I pay by card?

Diànzhǔ ： Duìbuqǐ ， wǒmen zhǐ shōu xiànjīn .
店主 ：对不起，我们 只 收 现金。

Seller: Sorry, we only accept cash.

Coco : Qǐng gěi wǒ fāpiào .
58 Coco：请 给 我 发票。

Coco: Would you please give me a receipt?

Diànzhǔ : Jiāo fèi hòu , dào zǒngfúwùtái kāi fāpiào .
店主：交费后，到 总服务台开 发票。

Seller: You can get a receipt from the Service Counter after payment.

Tips 9

Small Commodities Stores in Beijing

There are many small commodities stores around Beijing. The most famous ones are Tianqiao Small Commodities Store (at No. 22 Yongnei Ave., Chongwen District), Tianyi Market (at No. 259 Fuwai Ave., Xicheng District), Tianyu Small Commodities Store (at No. 10 East Tuanjiehu Rd., Chaoyang District), Tianyou Small Commodities Store (at 54 Baishiqiao Rd., Haidian District), Tianxing Small Commodities Store (at No. 16 North Dongzhimen Rd., Dongcheng District), Jiayi Plaza (at No. A3 Xinyuan Nanlu Rd., Chaoyang District), Golden Five-star Wholesale Market (at No. 18 Xueyuan Nanlu Rd., Haidian District) and etc.

UNIT 10

Chuántǒng Gōngyìpǐndiàn
传统 工艺品店
At a Traditional Arts & Crafts Store

Coco ： Zhèxiē xiǎo rénr zhēn yǒuyìsi ！
⑸⑼ Coco：这些 小人儿 真 有意思！

Coco: These small figures are so cute!

yǒuqù
有趣 interesting
kě'ài
可爱 lovely
hǎowánr
好玩儿 fun

Diànzhǔ： Shì ba ， zhè shì miànrénr .
店主：是吧，这是面人儿。

Shopkeeper: Yes, they are. They are dough figurines.

Coco ： Zhèxiē piàoliang de wáwa shì shénme?
⑥⓪ Coco：这些 漂亮 的娃娃是 什么？

Coco: What do you call these beautiful dolls?

Diànzhǔ： Zhè shì juànrénr ， yǒu yìqiān duō nián lìshǐ le .
店主 ：这是绢人儿，有 一千 多 年历史了。

Shopkeeper: They are called silk figurines, and have a history of over a thousand years.

Coco : Zhōngguó de Bābǐ Wáwa ! Wǒ yào mǎi yí ge sònggěi
61 Coco : 中国 的芭比娃娃！我 要 买一个送给
wǒ nǚ'ér .
我女儿。

érzi
儿子 son
háizi
孩子 kid
péngyou de háizi
朋友 的孩子 friend's kid

Coco: Chinese Barbie dolls!
I'll buy one for my daughter.

Diànzhǔ : Nín kànkan yào nǎge .
店主 ：您 看看 要哪个。
Shopkeeper: Which one would you like?

Coco : Zhège kěyǐ gěi wǒ zuò yí ge ma?
62 Coco：这个可以给我做一个吗？

Coco: Can you make one for me?

jiǎn
剪 cut

Diànzhǔ : Dāngrán kěyǐ . Wǒ gěi nín jiǎn ge húdié ba .
店主：当然可以。我给您剪个蝴蝶吧。

Shopkeeper: Of course. I shall cut a butterfly for you.

xiǎo gǒu
小狗 puppy
xiǎo māo
小猫 kitten
lǎohǔ
老虎 tiger

Coco : Zhège nán bu nán? Jiāojiao wǒ ba .
⑥③ Coco：这个难不难？教教我吧。

Coco: Is it difficult? Please teach me how to do it.

Diànzhǔ : Lái , wǒ jiāo nín yí ge jiǎndān de .
店主：来，我教您一个简单的。

Shopkeeper: OK. Let me teach you a simple one.

Coco ： Zhōngguójié wǒ xiǎng duō mǎi jǐ ge， néng bu
⑭ Coco：中国结 我 想 多 买几个，能不
néng piányi diǎnr ？
能便宜点儿？

dǎ ge zhé
打个折 give me a discount

Coco: I'd like to buy more Chinese knots. Could you reduce the price?

Diànzhǔ： Mǎi shí ge sòng yí ge .
店主：买十个送一个。
Shopkeeper: Buy ten and you can get one free.

Diànzhǔ : Zhēnzhū shǒuliàn , zìjǐ dài huò sòng rén dōu kěyǐ .
店主：珍珠手链，自己戴或送人都可以。
Shopkeeper: You can wear these pearl bracelets yourself or give them out as gifts.

Coco : Nà wǒ xuǎn jǐ ge ba .
⑮ Coco：那我选几个吧。
Coco: Then I'll choose some.

tiāo
挑 select

Tips 10

Paper Cuts and Silk Figurines

Chinese paper cutting is a unique and traditional folk art with a long history. Normally, papercuttings feature folk stories or patterns that bring good luck and expel evil. To make a silk figurine, one first puts together the iron wires for the figurine's ody and limbs. After that, cotton and paper pieces are used to fill in the body. Each step in making a figurine requires exquisite workmanship. It takes more than a month for one person to finish the process, and up to two or three months for finishing a complex figurine.

UNIT 11

Jiùhuò Shìchǎng
旧货 市场
At a Folk Culture Market

Coco： Zhè jiàn cíqì shì zhēn de háishi fǎng de？
⑥⑥ Coco：这件瓷器是真的还是仿的？

Coco: Is this piece of porcelain genuine or reproductive?

yùqì
玉器 jade
tóngqì
铜器 copperware

Diànyuán： Zhè jiàn shì gāofǎng de， hé zhēn de yíyàng．
店员：这件是高仿的，和真的一样。

Salesclerk: This is a quality reproduction, that looks just like the genuine one.

Coco ： Zhèxiē wǒ bú tài xǐhuan ， háiyǒu bié de ma？
⑥⑦ Coco：这些我不太喜欢，还有别的吗？

Coco: I don't like these. Do you have anything else?

Diànyuán： Zhè shì zhēn de Qīngcháo de ， sānqiān kuài .
店员：这是真的清朝的，3000 块。

Salesclerk: This is a genuine piece from the Qing Dynasty; it costs 3000 *kuai*.

Tángcháo
唐朝 Tang
Sòngcháo
宋朝 Song
Míngcháo
明朝 Ming

Coco : Zhème guì , kāi wánxiào ba .
⑥⑧ Coco：这么贵，开 玩笑吧。

Coco: That's so expensive, are you kidding?

Diànyuán : Hēhe , yì fēn qián yì fēn huò .
店员 ：呵呵，一分 钱一分 货。

Salesclerk: No, you get what you pay for.

Coco ： Wǒ xiǎng zài kètīng li guà fú zì-huà .
⑥⑨ Coco：我 想 在客厅里挂幅字画。

Coco: I would like to get
a calligraphy painting
for my living room.

shānshuǐhuà
山水画 landscape painting
huāniǎohuà
花鸟画 flower and bird painting
rénwùhuà
人物画 figure painting

Diànyuán： Zhèxiē dōu shì línmó míngjiā de .
店员 ：这些 都 是临摹名家的。

Salesclerk: These are all copy paintings of masterpieces.

Coco ： Yǒu dāngdài huàjiā de ma？
⑦⓪ Coco：有 当代 画家的吗？

shūfǎjiā
书法家 calligraphers

Coco: Do you have any works by contemporary painters?

Diànyuán ： Zhè fú xiàndài zuòpǐn ， háiyǒu shēngzhí kōngjiān ne .
店员 ：这幅现代作品，还有 升值 空间呢。
Salesclerk: This is a piece of modern art, which will increase in value.

Coco : Wǒ chángcháng kànjiàn zhège zì , zhè shì shénme zì ?
⑪ Coco：我 常常 看见这个字，这是什么字？

Coco: I often come across this character. What does it mean?

Diànyuán : Zhège zì shì "fú" , xìngfú de yìsi .
店员 ：这个字是“福”，幸福的意思。

Salesclerk: It is *fu*, which means happiness.

Coco : Zhè shì gǔdài de jiājù ma?
⑦② Coco：这是古代的家具吗？

Coco: Are these ancient furniture?

chuáng
床 beds
guìzi
柜子 cabinets
zhuōzi
桌子 tables
yǐzi
椅子 chairs

Diànyuán : Shì ya . Nín kànkan zhè gōngyì .
店员 ：是呀。您看看这工艺。

Salesclerk: Yes, they are. Look at the craftsmanship.

Tips 11

How to Identify Genuine and Fake Jade

Step 1. To observe the shine and luster. Real jade, either translucent or opaque, is always shiny. Also, it normally has tiny impurities or floccules in it. Fake jade has a faded luster, and the color is dull and dark. Sometimes they will contain air bubbles.

Step 2. To weigh in the hand. Real jade is dense, while fake jade is light.

Step 3. To listen to the sound. Hang the jade on a string and knock it lightly against something hard. The real jade will let off a long, clear ring, while the fake jade will make a short dull sound.

UNIT 12

Jiē BiānBàotíng
街边 报亭
At a Newspaper Stand

Coco : Jīntiān de "Zhōngguó Rìbào" hái yǒu ma?
⑦③ Coco：今天的《中国 日报》还有吗？

Coco: Do you still have today's *China Daily*?

Bàotíng lǎobǎn : Yǒu. Yí kuài wǔ.
报亭 老板：有。一块 五。

Vendor: Yes. One fifty please.

Coco : Yīngwénbǎn de "Cáifù" zázhì lái le ma?
⑭ Coco：英文版的《财富》杂志来了吗?

Coco: Has the English version of *Fortune* come out?

Botíng lǎobǎn : Hái méiyǒu . Qǐng nín zhōuyī lái ba .
报亭老板：还没有。请您周一来吧。

Vendor: Not yet. It will come out on Monday.

zhōu'èr
周二 Tuesday
zhōusān
周三 Wednesday
zhōusì
周四 Thursday
zhōuwǔ
周五 Friday
zhōuliù
周六 Saturday
zhōurì
周日 Sunday

Coco : Lǎobǎn, Yídòng de chōngzhíkǎ.
⑺ Coco：老板，移动的充值卡。

Liántōng
联通 China Unicom
Diànxìn
电信 China Telecom

Coco: Please give me one recharge card for China Mobile.

Bàotíng lǎobǎn : Wǔshí de háishi yìbǎi de ?
报亭 老板： 50 的还是 100 的？
Vendor: 50 or 100 yuan?

Coco ： Yìbǎi de . Zhège zěnme yòng?
⑯ Coco：100 的。这个怎么用？

Coco: 100 please. How do I use it?

chōng zhí
充值 recharge
cāozuò
操作 operate

Bàotíng lǎobǎn： Nín bōdǎ kǎ shang de diànhuà， yǒu yǔyīn tíshì .
报亭老板：您拨打卡上的电话，有语音提示。

Vendor: You can dial the number on the card and then follow the voice instructions.

Coco : Duìbuqǐ , wǒ méi tīng qīngchu .
⑺ Coco：对不起，我没 听 清楚。

míngbai
明白 follow
dǒng
懂 know

Coco: I'm sorry. I do not understand this.

Bàotíng lǎobǎn : Nín dǎ zhège diànhuà jiù zhīdào le .
报亭 老板：您打这个 电话 就知道了。

Vendor: You can dial this phone number to get an explanation.

Coco : Nǐ bāng wǒ chōngshàng, hǎo ma?
⑱ Coco : 你 帮 我 充 上 , 好 吗?

Coco: Could you please recharge it for me?

Bàotíng lǎobǎn : Méi wèntí ... Chōng hǎo le .
报亭 老板 : 没问题…… 充 好了。

Vendor: No problem.… Done!

Tips 12

Recharge Cards

China Mobile, China Unicom and China Telecom are the three mobile suppliers in China. Accordingly there are three types of rechargeable mobile phone cards. Attention should be paid before purchasing these cards. The recharge phone numbers of China Mobile, China Unicom and China Telecom are respectively 13800138000, 10011 and 11888. You can dial the specific phone number and then follow the voice instructions to input the code on the card to recharge a mobile phone, or you can ask the recharge card seller for help.

UNIT 13

Huāhuì Shìchǎng
花卉 市场
At a Flower Market

Coco： Lǎobǎn， zhè huā jiào shénme? Zhēn xiāng a.
⑲ Coco：老板，这花叫什么？真香啊。

Coco: What's the name of this flower? It smells so good.

Diànzhǔ： Zhè shì yèláixiāng.
店主：这是夜来香。

Seller: It is called evening primrose.

xūnyīcǎo
薰衣草 lavender
yějúhuā
野菊花 wild chrysanthemum
mòlì
茉莉 jasmine
shuǐxiān
水仙 narcissus

Coco : Wǒ xiǎng mǎi ge bǎi zài kètīng de lǜsè zhíwù .

⑧⓪ Coco：我 想 买个摆在客厅的绿色植物。

Coco: I'd like to buy a green plant for my living room.

wòshì
卧室 bedroom
fàntīng
饭厅 dining room
bàngōngshì
办公室 office

Diànzhǔ : Diàolán búcuò , kěyǐ jìnghuà kōngqì .

店主：吊兰不错，可以净化 空气。

Seller: The spider plant will suit you. It can purify the air in the room.

Lúhuì
芦荟 aloe
Guībèizhú
龟背竹 ceriman
Fùguìzhú
富贵竹 lucky bamboo
Lǜluó
绿萝 scindapsus
Tiěshù
铁树 sago cycad

Coco ： Lǎobǎn， pénjǐng zuì dī duōshao qián？
⑧① Coco：老板，盆景最低多少钱？

zuì shǎo
最少 minimum

Coco: What is the best price for the miniature trees?

Lǎo diànzhǔ： Xiǎo pén de bāshí yuán， dà pén de yìbǎi yuán．
老店主：小盆的 80 元，大盆的 100 元。
Old Vendor: 80 for the small ones and 100 for the big ones.

Coco : Wǒ mǎi zhème duō , yōuhuì diǎnr ba .
⑧② Coco：我买这么多，优惠点儿吧。

Coco: I have bought so many, I should get a better price.

Lǎo diànzhǔ : Bù jiǎngjià . Búguò , wǒmen miǎnfèi sòng huò .
老店主：不讲价。不过，我们免费送货。
Old Vendor: We have no discount. But the delivery is free.

Coco ： Néng bu néng huòdào-fùkuǎn？
⑧③ Coco：能不能 货到付款？

Coco: Can I pay on delivery?

Lǎo diànzhǔ： Kěyǐ . Xiānjiāo wǔshí yuán dìngjīn .
老店主：可以。先交 50 元 定金。

Old Vendor: Yes. Please pay a deposit of 50 yuan now, though.

Coco : Wǒ míngtiān shàngwǔ zài jiā děngzhe .
84 Coco：我 明天 上午 在家等着 。

zhōngwǔ
中午 noon
xiàwǔ
下午 afternoon

Coco: I'll wait for it tomorrow morning.

Lǎo diànzhǔ : Hǎo , sòng shí huì gěi nín dǎ diànhuà .
老店主：好，送时会给您打电话。

Old Vendor: Okay. I'll call you when I'm arriving at your house.

Lǎo diànzhǔ： Zhè zhī méigui sònggěi nín， huānyíng xià cì guānglín.
老店主：这支玫瑰送给您，欢迎下次光临。

Old Vendor: This long stemmed rose is for you. Come again.

bǎihé 百合 lily
yùjīnxiāng 郁金香 tulip
kāngnǎixīn 康乃馨 carnation

Coco： Nǐ zhēn hǎo. Xièxie.
⑧⑤ Coco：你真好。谢谢。

Coco: That is very kind of you. Thank you.

Tips 13

Feature Flowers in China

China has many feature flowers such as peony, osmanthus, lotus, camellia, cuckoo, orchid, Chinese peony and so on. The Chinese people prefer potted flowers to the cut flowers that westerners' like. Various potted flowers are put in living rooms, bedrooms, dining rooms and offices, to decorate and lighten up the rooms.

UNIT 14

Biànlìdiàn
便利店
At a Convenience Store

Coco： Qǐngwèn， yǒu méiyǒu wú táng bǐnggān？
⑧⑥ Coco：请问，有没有无糖饼干？

Coco: Excuse me. Do you have sugar free biscuits?

dàngāo
蛋糕 cakes
miànbāo
面包 bread
niúnǎi
牛奶 milk
suānnǎi
酸奶 yoghurt

Diànyuán： Yǒu. Zài zhèbian.
店员：有。在这边。

Salesclerk: Yes. They are over here.

Coco : Nǐ hǎo . Yì píng lǜchá .
⑧⑦ Coco：你好。一瓶<u>绿茶</u>。

Coco: Hello. A bottle of <u>green tea</u> please.

kělè
可乐 Cola
kuàngquánshuǐ
矿泉水 mineral water
yǐnliào
饮料 drink

Diànyuán : Nàbian bīngxiāng li , qǐng nín zì qǔ .
店员：那边 冰箱 里，请您自取。

Salesclerk: It's over there in the fridge. Please help yourself.

Coco： Láojià， qǐng guòlai yíxià。
⑧⑧ Coco：劳驾，请过来一下。

Coco: Excuse me. Can you please come and help me.

Diànyuán： Nín yǒu shénme xūyào？
店员：您有什么需要？

Clerk: How can I help you?

Coco : Zhège guàntou shì bu shì guòqī le ?
⑧⑨ Coco：这个罐头是不是过期了？

Coco: Has this canned food expired?

niúnǎi
牛奶 milk
guǒjiàng
果酱 jam
miànbāo
面包 bread
xiāngcháng
香肠 sausage

Diànyuán : Méiyǒu, zhè shì shēngchǎn rìqī .
店员：没有，这是生产日期。

Salesclerk: No, it hasn't. This is the date of production.

Coco : Qǐngwèn, zhèr de píjiǔ néng tuì píngr ma?
⑨⓪ Coco：请问，这儿的啤酒能退瓶儿吗？

Coco: Excuse me, do you accept empty beer bottles?

Diànyuán : Wǒmen zhèr bú tuì, duìmiàn de shāngdiàn kěyǐ tuì.
店员：我们这儿不退，对面的商店可以退。
Salesclerk: No, we don't. You can go to the store across the road though, they accept.

Coco : Gǒu liáng guàntou yǒu ma?
⑨① Coco：狗粮罐头有吗？

Māo
猫 cat

Coco: Have you got canned dog food?

Diànyuán : Niúròuwèi, jīròuwèi, yángròuwèi de dōu yǒu.
店员：牛肉味、鸡肉味、羊肉味的都有。

Salesclerk: Yes, we have got all types: beef, chicken and mutton.

Diànyuán : Língqián qǐng diǎnhǎo .
店员 ：零钱 请 点好。

Salesclerk: Check your change.

Coco : Zhènghǎo , xièxie .
92 Coco ：正好 ，谢谢。

Coco: It's correct. Thanks.

Coco : Zhèli tígōng xìnyòngkǎ huán kuǎn fúwù ma?
⑨③ Coco：这里提供信用卡还款服务吗？

tíkuǎnjī qǔ xiàn
提款机取现 withdraw cash from the ATM
gōngjiāokǎ chōng zhí
公交卡充值 recharge my public transport IC card
dài jiǎo diànfèi
代缴电费 pay my electricity bill
fùyìn
复印 use a photocopier
dàichōng jiāojuǎn
代冲胶卷 develop film

Coco: Can I pay off my credit card here?

Diànyuán : Dāngrán! Wǒmen tígōng duō zhǒng biàn-mín fúwù.
店员：当然！我们提供多种便民服务。
Salesclerk: Sure! We provide many different services.

Tips 14

Services offered at Convenience Stores

Convenience stores, characterized by their close location to communities, and warm and attentive service, are popular among the people. Besides daily necessities and food and drinks, some convenience stores also sell fast or cooked food. In some stores people can even deposit or withdraw money, send faxes, make photocopies, recharge their public transport IC cards, pay water, electricity and gas bills, as well as book train tickets, develop film and make phone calls.

UNIT 15

Shūdiàn
书店
At a Bookstore

Coco : Zhè shì zuì xīn de Běijīng dìtú ma?
94 Coco : 这是最新的北京地图吗?

Coco: Is this the latest Beijing Map?

zuì quán
最全 most comprehensive
zuì dà
最大 biggest

Diànyuán : Shì de .
店员 : 是的。

Salesclerk: Yes, it is.

Coco : Wǒ xiǎng kànkan lǚyóu de shū . Néng gěi wǒ jièshào jǐ běn ma?
⑨⑤ Coco：我 想 看看旅游的书。能 给 我 介 绍 几本 吗？

měishí
美食 food
měiróng
美容 make-up
zhōngyī
中医 TCM
xué Hànyǔ
学汉语 Chinese language learning

Coco: I am looking for books on travel. Could you suggest anything for me?

Diànyuán : Zhè běn búcuò , háiyǒu hěn duō zhàopiàn .
店员 ：这 本 不错，还有 很 多 照片 。

Clerk: This one is quite good, and there are quite a lot of pictures.

Coco： Qǐng bāng wǒ zhǎo yíxià "Dāngdài Zhōngwén".
⑯ Coco：请帮我找一下《当代中文》。

Coco: Would you please find the book *Contemporary Chinese* for me?

Diànyuán： Wǒ bāng nín dào nàbian de diànnǎo chá yíxià.
店员：我帮您到那边的电脑查一下。

Clerk: I'll check for you on the computer.

Diànyuán : Nín kànkan zhège diànzǐ cídiǎn , hěn fāngbiàn .
店员 ：您看看这个电子词典，很 方便。

shíyòng
实用 practical

Clerk: Have a look at this electronic dictionary. It is very convenient.

Coco : Wǒ yǐjīng mǎiguo le .
⑰ Coco ：我已经买过了。

Coco: I already have one.

Tips 15

Well-known Bookstores and Online Bookstores Around Beijing

The most well known bookstores in Beijing include Xidan Beijing Books Building, the Zhongguancun Book Building, Wangfujing Bookstore, Wangfujing Foreign Languages Bookstore and the Gongti Foreign Languages Bookstore as well as many others.

Now more and more readers prefer online bookstores as it is more convenient for them to search the book titles and find better prices, as well as saving them the time and energy of having to go to the stores. Dangdang, Joyo Amazon and Weilan are the most notable online bookstores.

UNIT 16

Wǎngshang Gòuwù
网上 购物
Online Shopping

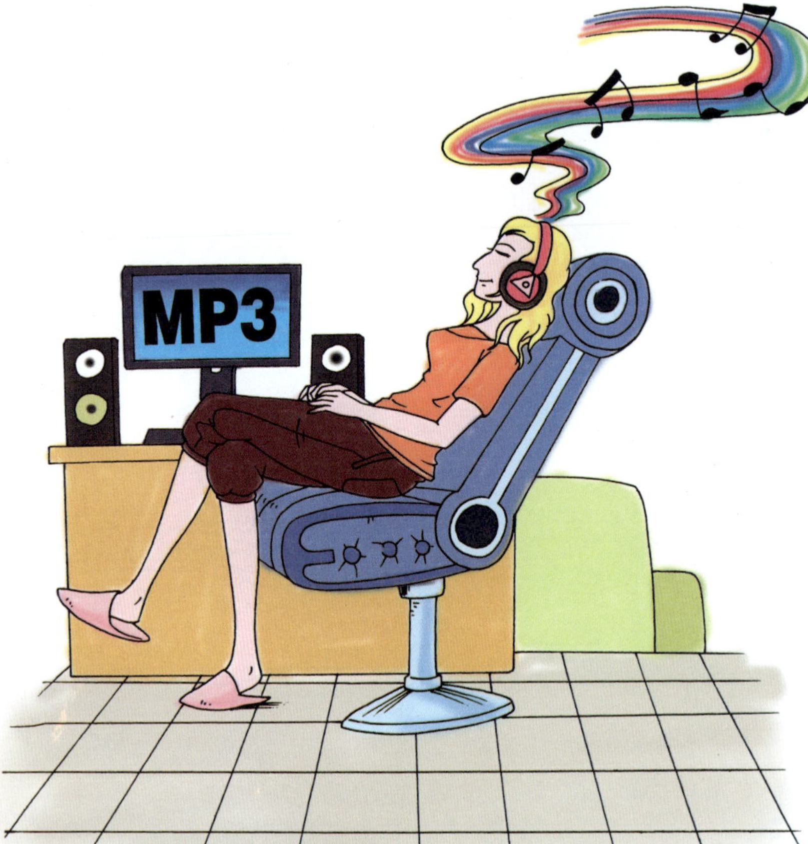

Coco : Wǒ xiǎng mǎi ge MP3 . Fùjìn hǎoxiàng méiyǒu diànzǐ shāngchéng .
⑱ Coco：我想买个MP3。附近好像没有电子商城。

Coco: I'd like to buy an MP3 player, but there are no electronics stores nearby.

Péngyou : Nǐ shàngwǎng mǎi , yòu piányi yòu fāngbiàn .
朋友：你上网买，又便宜又方便。

Friend: You can buy one on the Internet.

Coco ： Lái Zhōngguó yǐhòu hái méi zài wǎngshang gòuwù ne ！
⑨⑨ Coco：来中国以后还没在网上购物呢！

Coco: I have not tried online shopping since I came to China.

Péngyou： Hěn jiǎndān， wǒ bāng nǐ ．
朋友：很简单，我帮你。

Friend: It's easy. Let me help you.

Yóudìyuán ： Qǐngwèn shì Coco jiā ma ?
邮递员 ： 请问 是 Coco 家吗？

Postman: Is this Coco's home?

Coco ： Duì . Wǒ jiù shì .
100 Coco ：对。我就是。

Coco: Yes, it is.

Yóudìyuán : Zhè shì nín mǎi de MP3 . Zài zhèr qiān zì .
邮递员：这是您买的MP3。在这儿签字。

Postman: Here is your MP3 player. Please sign your name here.

Coco : Zhème kuài jiù dào la ! Xièxie .
101 Coco：这么快就到啦！谢谢。

Coco: That was so quick. Thank you.

Tips 16

Online Shopping

Buying online is growing more and more popular among young people, especially for clothes, small electronic products, stationery and sports goods. It is recommended that consumers choose trusted and established shopping websites, and reliable web stores that have had good evaluations. When making payments, consumers should choose to pay using a third party go-between and should not disclose their login and passwords to the sellers.

漫画汉语101句（美食篇）
Chinese 101 in Cartoons (For Eating Out)

▶ 汉英 Chinese-English edition
ISBN 9787802059760
By Hou Kun
145×210 mm，123pp，0.26kg
¥46.0

- 适合汉语水平为零起点、对中国美食感兴趣的汉语学习者。
- 选取风味餐厅、小吃店等各种场景中常用的汉语会话101 句。
- 常用句式给出多种可替换词，一句衍生多句。
- 采用轻松活泼的漫画形式辅助学习汉语。
- 采用小贴士形式介绍中国经典美食和美食文化。
- Designed specially for beginners of Chinese language who basically have no command of Chinese, and are interested in Chinese food.
- 101 commonly-used conversational expressions for people to use in restaurants and eateries.
- Each sentence pattern is supplemented with multiple substitutive elements.
- Lively cartoons are provided as aids for learning.
- Tips are provided on typical Chinese dishes and food culture.

漫画汉语101句（旅游篇）
Chinese101 in Cartoons (For Travelers)

▶ 汉英 Chinese-English edition
ISBN 9787802004566
By Zhang Jing
145×210mm，128pp，0.26kg
¥45.00

- 本书为“漫画汉语系列”读物之一，针对汉语水平为零起点的外国来华游客的需要，选取旅途中各种场景下常用汉语会话101 句，并采用轻松活泼的漫画形式予以解读，另配MP3 格式光盘提供标准读音，让汉语变得易学易会，让来华游客轻松掌握简单的汉语日常用语。
- This book is designed for foreign travelers in China who basically have no command of Chinese. 101 most commonlyused conversational expressions are chosen for travelers to get around. Each sentence pattern is supplemented with multiple substitutive elements. Lively cartoons serve as aids for learning.

漫画汉语101句（CEO篇）
Chinese 101 in Cartoons (For CEOs)

▶ 汉英 Chinese-English editon
ISBN 9787802004085
By Zhang Jing
145×210mm，132pp，0.26kg
¥45.00

- 适合汉语水平为零起点的外国企业管理者或商务人士。
- 选取在华商务活动中各种场景下常用汉语会话101 句。
- 常用句式给出多种可替换词，一句衍生多句。
- 采用轻松活泼的漫画形式辅助学习汉语。
- 文中穿插小贴士介绍中国经济环境、文化常识及风俗习惯等。
- Intended for foreign business executives who basically have no command of Chinese.
- 101 commonly-used conversational expressions for situations encountered when doing business in China.
- Each sentence pattern is supplemented with multiple substitutive elements.
- Lively cartoons as aids for learning.
- Tips on economic, cultural knowledge and local custom are included.

漫画汉语101句（学生篇）
Chinese 101 in Cartoons (For Students)

▶ 汉英 Chinese-English edition
ISBN 9787802006287
By Zhang Jing
145×210 mm，119pp，0.26kg
¥45.00

- 适合汉语水平为零起点的外国留学生。
- 选取校园生活中各种场景下学生常用的汉语会话101句。
- 常用句式给出多种可替换词，一句衍生多句。
- 采用轻松活泼的漫画形式辅助学习汉语。
- 采用小贴士形式介绍中国学生的学习、生活状况，以及校园幽默。
- Designed specially for foreign students in China who basically have no command of Chinese.
- 101 commonly-used conversational expressions for students to use on campus.
- Each sentence pattern is supplemented with multiple substitutive elements.
- Lively cartoons are provided as aids for learning.
- Tips are provided on Chinese students' study and life, together with campus humor.

责任编辑：付　华
英文编辑：韩　敏
封面设计：古　手
印刷监制：佟汉冬

图书在版编目（CIP）数据

漫画汉语 101 句．购物篇：汉英对照／侯琨，史文华编著．—北京：华语教学出版社，2010
ISBN 978-7-80200-938-7

I.①漫… II.①侯… ②史… III.①汉语—口语—对外汉语教学—教材 IV.①H195.4

中国版本图书馆 CIP 数据核字（2010）第 132227 号

漫画汉语 101 句（购物篇）

侯 琨 史文华 编著
韩芙芸 译
千秋叶工作室 插图
*

华语教学出版社有限责任公司出版
（中国百万庄大街 24 号 邮政编码 100037）
电话：(86)10-68320585
传真：(86)10-68326333
网址：www.sinolingua.com.cn
电子信箱：hyjx@sinolingua.com.cn
北京外文印刷厂印刷
2011 年（32 开）第一版
（汉英）
ISBN 978-7-80200-938-7
定价：49.00 元